I0201047

Kissed By Words

The Prelude

A. I. R.

Kissed By Words:The Prelude

Kissed By Words: The Prelude

COPYRIGHT ©2014 Andre Rogers (A. I. R.)

All rights reserved. No part of this book may be used or reproduced in any manner whatsoever without written permission except in the case of brief quotations embodied in critical articles or reviews. For information address BlaqRayn Publishing & Promotions, 134 Andrew Drive, NC 27320

Printed in the United States of America

ISBN-10:0692026096

ISBN-13:978-0-692-02609-0

Printed by Createspace in 2014

Published by BlaqRayn Publishing in 2014

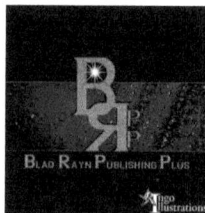

Kissed By Words:

The Prelude

A. I. R.

Kissed By Words:The Prelude

He Says More

You better believe in me
Cause in time you'll need me
Life into you I have breathed
Through my Word you shall take
heed
For I am filled with jealousy
When you live a life full of hypocrisy
You will receive a lot not just for
show
From whom all blessings flow
My kingdom will be your safe have
You are saved in-spite of all you're
misbehaving
I will answer that knock at the door
Stay with me still He Says More

Whom in heaven but you
Give me praise in all that you do
I am with you always
Even to the end of age
I have no pleasures in the death of
the wicked

Kissed By Words:The Prelude

The Coming of the Son has been
predicted
For why should you die O'house of
Israel?
By grace through faith all shall be
healed
Worship puts God at the center of
our vision
Wisdom knowledge understanding as
Well as hope and humility is the key
to the ignition
I know your works see I have set
before you an open door
Aren't we blessed He Says More

Love Ya Mom

I know things haven't been like they
should
But I know you have done the best
you could
If I could turn the hands of time I
would
The nurturing, care and security from
birth
Is the best thing I could have here on
this earth?
You've done a good job to raise a
gentleman
I thank you for that I owe you my
right hand
Having someone else as a mother I
couldn't stand
You're due more treasures in all the
land
To show my gratitude has always
been my plan
I appreciate the life you have given
me

Know this I'm saying these things
sincerely
Hold your head high as it can go
Cause you've done well that's all I
know
Nothing could break this bond, not
even the Atomic Bomb
You know why cause I Love You Mom!

Coach B.

A
A man that stands up with humility
A man with hope, faith, and integrity
The only guy I know deserving of
sincerity
He said son you can go places if you
strive
Don't rob, steal and hustle to get by
Jails, cemeteries, and prison filled
with men like me
But you know they don't have to be
All he wants is for us to be somebody
I know you got potential to do a great
thing
But it takes more than merely getting
that bling
You got to fight the big fight
You got to struggle through the
battles fought
You can't get up for school but you
can stay up all night

Learn what you can learn teach what
you've been taught
I always said I never met a hero
Someone I can always say been real
and not a zero
A man enduring the pains of trials
and tribulations
An upright and honest person a real
revelation
I guess what I'm trying to say you see
Is man up and ok, I was listening
Thanks Coach B.
Inspired by Coach Baldwin

What We Are Called

For awhile anyone of African descent
Was considered as indecent
We were known as slaves and rock
throwers
We were called the colored so our
expectations would be lowered
In the south they named us jungle
bunnies, porch monkey, and gator
bait
Labeled like savaged beasts that had
escaped
Jody is that black guy going out the
back door
But us Jigga Boo's were the ones
that's adored
On the west coast they gave us better
more common names
Like spooks and spades
And that's the thanks we get for all of
the accomplishments that we have
undeniably made

Kissed By Words:The Prelude

We didn't' have any but our debts are
paid
Now you go down in the lower mid
west
The names they gave us you couldn't
guess
Tar-babies, yard apes, jigs and
coons...
But Black America is still out of tune
We even have names in other
languages like Moolie and Miate'
And they make the same wages yet
and still they stuck on the years
before pages
Reparations now is what I say
Still haven't gotten compensated to
this day
Our ways of living have always been
rough
But that's what makes us thugs tough
It has been indented in our mind
state
That we hoodlums and hood-rats are
irate

Kissed By Words:The Prelude

Our own kind calls us nigger and gang
banger
And just like us they put their clothes
on a hanger
I guess there will never be a way to
suppress
Mine and my studious African
Americans anger
They were mad like we made them
work for free
We didn't buy tickets to come over
across seas
All I want is a say over here and
equality
Is that so much to ask for
I guess so since we now use the front
door
They clutch their purses
And supply us with all type of curses
We are the second largest minority
Africa is the richest country
But the poorest on the contrary
Did they pick cotton in the hot fields?
No so they can't say they know how
we feel

Kissed By Words:The Prelude

When I say we I mean as a whole
Just to called be called by my name
properly is a goal
Call us what you want
We still stand strong on the home
front
Even when you're rich and famous or
blackballed
Don't forget "What We Are Called"

What They Are Called

You have all types of people
Some maybe a little more feeble
As times progressed so did their
names
Like spaghetti wrappers, taco
benders, they aren't all from Spain
The Espanol, Dago's, pepper pickers
and jungle rats
They work hard just to be hassled and
called wet backs
The world is ever so horribly
corrupted, that's no lie
Not because of chinks, gooks, the
one's called slant eyes
They are no better or less than us,
they work too to get by
But the snow bunnies, "The Man"
them pink-toed hicks
Still segregate why don't they just
give up and quit

Kissed By Words:The Prelude

Them people worked hard and the reward Spik….
Oh! Then you got the Irish who speak Gaelic

I don't know why them hippies, crackers, them pale faces
Don't fathom or can't come to reality that these aren't color cases
Those sand niggers and rag-heads are just different races
The Jews also known as Kikes, were persecuted because of culture
By those skin heads and krauts them vultures
Now in this new world people who practice hate
Aryan, sheets, and national socialist's people's party are irate
Protested, unjust beliefs and that's no debate
In other parts of the world people was called wops
Men and women of polish descent were considered Pollocks

Kissed By Words:The Prelude

As the days go by I ponder why this
place is unfair
How is it that not one person really
cares

In Australia no matter what we're
called Septics
And there is nothing we can do but
except it
Them slave traders rant and rave
But they never was beaten or had to
be enslaved
Because of their color or just because
they misbehave
Don't get me wrong I have a lot of
white friends
It's just the home you grew up in not
the color of your skin
I feel that as human beings we are
misguided
And that's how races and minorities
collided
Some way or another we have to get
rid of bigotry

Kissed By Words:The Prelude

Unity, equality, and treated justly is
my theory
People seemed to ignore the fact that
we bleed the same
We are different colors and shouldn't
be put to shame

I was born Black but am I to be the
blame
And so I think racialism and
antagonism is lame
We shouldn't be judged because of
miscegenation
Maybe it is just a matter of
misinterpretation
Equality wherever you live should be
indisputable
Freedom and fairness seem to be
incomprehensible
When you walk out into the world
you should be ostentatious
Fake it until you make it isn't that
stupendous
So all in all, these are just a few
reasons why

Kissed By Words:The Prelude

Mankind will certainly unintentionally
fall
But not just because of "What They
Are Called"

Beautiful to Me

The wind beneath my wings
The causation why I sing
The ladder to my high hopes
My ski's on the worlds slopes
The waves in my ocean you see
Those are the basis for you being
Beautiful to ME

The twinkle in mine eyes
The reason I can get by
The joy in my happy life
The worth in having a wife
The furnace to my heat
The one who holds the key

Can't you understand why you are so?
Beautiful To Me

The fruit of my tree
The cushion in my seat
The sugar in my sweets

Kissed By Words:The Prelude

Somebody I thought I'd never meet
The pulse to my steady heartbeat
Now that's certainly why you are
"Beautiful To Me"

Poetry

An indistinct cry from your mind
Something to express my feelings as a
sign
Whenever I seem to get the time
A special kind of writing in rhythm
and rhyme
Poems are symbols of our own
expressions
Sometimes they may show images of
affections
To explain my extraordinary,
influential floe-try
I use shape and structure in my
"Poetry"

Those sound effects that you hear
Are what draws my readers near
The high rise and low fall of my words
My Thoughts are seen rather than
heard
Unlike a cowhand demands his herd

Kissed By Words:The Prelude

My feelings soar like the largest
winged bird
Although I may exaggerate a tad bit
But that's the only way I can explain
it
I have given you a mental picture
grim but never gory
This is how I learned to tell my life's
story
Through this simple thing called
"Poetry"

Shopping List

Into life's only store I go
What I'll come out with I don't know
I'm not press for time so I'll go slow
I need a job, a house, and a running
car
Got to get an education first, that will
take me far
Wisdom is also what I need to pickup
I have to get some faith to add to my
trust
Can't forget to get some knowledge
Oh I need a scholarship for a college
Now I got to get a wife and some kids
Let me see what is under this lid
Wow its Salvation now that I can't
miss
Well I think I have enough
understanding
So I can afford everything on my
"Shopping List"

Kissed By Words:The Prelude

What You Know

What you know about trepidation
that's fearful anxiety
Waiting to see the day when I will be
unlocked and free
What you know about them
Wednesday mystery meals
The day you eat everything there so
your stomach will fill
What you know about taking
paranoid schizo-pills
Chained and locked away so all your
dreams will be just thrills
What you know about those roll up
cigs
Smoking them while you work a 32
cent a a day gig
What you know about leaving behind
fatherless kids
That's one of the horrible deeds you
realize you did

What you know about flying jail cell
kites
So you can get zoo-zoos, wham
whams, and CD's that's tight
What you know about all them cell
block fights
Can't forget after ten there is no TV
or lights
What you know about praying to get
in heaven
Reading the Book that teaches me
about bread that's unleavened
What you know about a thing we call
three hots and a cot
In here you got no control over
whether it's cold or hot
Standing and eating at your everyday
spot
Learning the tricks of trade to get
some chop
This is real life not some prime time
television show
You can survive but it's all about who
and "What You Know"

Kissed By Words:The Prelude

Think...

Think before you speak
That won't make you weak
Do not think carnally
Even though it's done universally
Our thinking is synchronous
And that's what pairs us
Me and you think just alike
You don't realize it when they're in
your sight
Think again

Consider that when choosing a friend
I think we should think things over
Do we as people really need a
chauffeur?
I'll have to think about that
That's how you keep relationships in
tact
You and I think identical to each
other
And it don't have to be a cousin,
sister or brother

Kissed By Words:The Prelude

I think you should contemplate
Whether we'll be friends or we'll date
Are you thinking what I am thinking?
Is something in her eye or is she
winking
To learn more meditate on them
Without even a thought or a blink
Tell me so what do you "Think"

The Five P's

Life as you live it can be pleasurable
or painful
These consequences we suffer are
really a handful
To gain prosperity and longevity, gain
first, endurance
Tribulations will in the future,
produce perseverance
If I could I'd wipe all our problems
with a big tissue
I can't though, so we have to deal
with today's issues
Society is like a new disease that is
incurable
You make things so difficult they
become indecipherable
Nowadays everybody have a hard
time being pro-choice
But we don't have a problem getting
a divorce

In my eyes I feel they both wrong so
why procrastinate
Our kids are becoming more and
more profligate
Cause they're trying so hard to be
preponderate
Deep inside we as adults are all truly
in thrall
That's why at times we have that feel
of gall
In whatever you do always have a
little patience
Remember Prior Planning Prevents
Poor Performance
You want a change and some
productivity, seize,
Take heed please to "The Five P's"

The Lord Is There

In You O'Lord I put my trust
Let me never be put to shame
Your people need you to help us
We're sinners but the devil is to
blame

Make haste to help me
I'm poor and very needy
God we rest in your care
Because "The Lord is There"

You find in Him all that you need
You find in yourself great misery
God issued us a decree
Let it be done ever so diligently
The waters have come up to my neck
Save me O God my life is a wreck
On the inside looking out
On the outside looking in
You love me without a doubt
You have forgiven me for my sin

Kissed By Words:The Prelude

I'm never alone in the devils lair
You know why because Jehovah
Shammah "The Lord is There"

Children of Peace

Buffoons, welfare recipients, a joke
Forget the stereotypes, Dom Spiro
Sparrow
Cause while I breathe I hope
We don't believe in fairytales
But we put reliance on the many jails
Babe, baby, little ones, and infant
We are all someone's descendant
Just because we use hair grease
Don't mean we aren't Children of
Peace

We may not know how the silver-
spoon looks
We know what we've cleaned and
cooked
I'm talking about inherited wealth
I suppose you know what I mean
I'm talking about that money on the
shelf
I suppose you think I'm green

Don't worry I'm not mad
Actually I am veritably glad
We are optimistic, jovial and hurt no
more
Serenity is what we strive for
We praise undoubtedly
We are ever so lofty
We sing loudly
We blame thus softly
Don't taunt us please
Because we're Amani-Children of
Peace

Who Will Cry for the Little Boy

Will you cry for the little man?
Can you help him to understand?
Is it possible for his tree to bear fruits?
If so will it have good roots?
Will you give him something he can keep?
Do you kiss him and watch him sleep
Does he know everything will be alright?
Are you there when he awakes at night?
Is there a life for him to enjoy
Who will cry for the little boy?

Will he always be depressed?
Did you tell him what it means to be oppressed?
Tomorrow isn't promised to him
And today is such a big problem
It's a hard knock life I know this
Will he ever be someone to miss?
I can never tell if he's okay

Kissed By Words:The Prelude

I just tell him there will come a day
When he will receive his overdue pay
Stay strong little guy and pray
Will it be better if I buy him a toy?
Maybe but tell me honestly
"Who Will Cry for the Little Boy"

Soul Sistahs

Mahogany toned could turn any
heart to stone
Deep brown suga eyes that have seen
many things
Ebony skin with teeth when she
smiles bling
A precious hidden treasure lies within
her body
You are my new found business
called my chocolate factory
Hand in hand me and you could be as
one whole
Could she possibly be worth more
than platinum and gold
Smooth as sweet chocolate and thick
like caramel candy
Long luscious legs and intelligence
that comes in handy
Similar to a piece of toffee but a lot
stronger than coffee

A superb lustrous and good-natured
individual
A woman of intriguing fascination I
think I can handle
The way she talks she resembles a
beautiful pictcha
So whenever you see me in public
just call me mista
Cause I'm representing for my
elegant "Soul Sistah"

Are "Unthinkable"

The thoughts I have are unshakable
My infatuation with you is
memorable
Truthfully you are surely sensational
I have grown to believe the
unbelievable
My intentions have been very
honorable
Tell me do you think this bond we
have is
"Unbreakable"

One rare occasion I meet women so
Indispensable and also seemingly
adorable
When I'm with you I am extremely
comfortable
But when you are way it makes me
vulnerable
The wrongs are stupidly innumerable

I guarantee I'll show you I'm
remorseful and lovable
Now let it be known soul-mates are
"Unbreakable"

Am I speaking in simple ways of
parables?
Sometimes I feel our marrying was
and is
Implausible and too inconceivable
If I ever lost you it would be
unbearable
This love I've been diagnosed with is
incurable
My proposal no matter what is
indisputable
The yearning in my soul is inevitable
These emotions I have for my seat
are
Indescribable remember true
friendship and
Eternal loves are "Unbreakable"

Kissed By Words:The Prelude

Disbelief

Times of turmoil and trouble
Seemingly it comes twice-fold double
What is that I can do?
To relieve myself of this despair
How can I ever pull thru?
And be a man dapper and debonair
Low income and high cost
Struggling and striving to be the boss
Continually puts me at my wits end
It is blind to race, creed, or the color
of skin
When will this anguish cease to exist?
Feelings of vengeance how can you
resist
Cost of living and dying go hand and
hand
And yet they stand up and are a man
Women are like gas prices
Up then down but needed like
licenses

How can we reverse the effects of
failure?
Without being confronted with the
pain we endure
Be all you can be and you can
succeed
Into your life I have breathed
Be fruitful multiply in other words
breed
Knock and you shall be answered
Give in order to receive
All I need is faith enhancer
That way in His word I can take heed
I am still waiting for a sense relief
So I can disarm myself of this
"Disbelief"

Do You

Two hearts, two minds. In time got
together and intertwined
Did find one target one love and also
one aim
And came to know our paths were
truly the same
Setting time aside to learn from and
about each other
You supply all the comfort and
security like a loving mother
Sometimes we wonder about both of
our idiosyncrasies
But yet we still remain in one another
sexual fantasies
This is more than just some affair
d'amour or people who fancy
When we are near each other our
emotions and hearts fandango
As I look through those precious eyes
of yours I notice a romantic glow

You smile and say nice things and let
me know it's not just for show
Let's take a ride to our destination
the rainbow sky
I feel this connection but I really
don't' fathom why
I honestly think a blissful marriage
could keep us together like glue
Problems, there will be a few, I
believe we could handle them "Do
You"

Free

From the Underground Railroad to
the Freedom Rally
From Harriet Tubman and Rosa Parks
to working in a galley
From Frederick Douglas to a black
man named Medgar Evers
From the slave ships and cotton fields
to streets of terrors
From Martin Luther King and
Malcolm X to many mistakes and
errors

They saw many people suffering and
tried to heal it
They also saw a disease growing and
tried to kill it
Those men and women saw a war
and tried to stop it
They notice a mess in the streets and
tried to mop it

Once they realized the problems they
tried to solve them
Dr. King wanted rights for all of us not
just for him
I thank God that I wasn't around for
slavery
Tucked away and confined like
money in a treasury
Put behind you the outrage and take
heed
To the words of the ones who caused
us to be "Free"

We have struggled for way too long
Comin fo' to carry me home
She said let my people go because
she wasn't alone
It's because of these people I have a
dream
They're the reason why we see
through the smoke screen
Out of the hands of bondage and
imprisonment
Take a long look at how our freedom
has been spent

Kissed By Words:The Prelude

They taught me not to follow but
always lead
That's what I call male and female
maturity
In conclusion enjoy the time we have
to be "Free"

Grave Sights

Listening to the sounds of ghoulish
frights
Six-feet deep but everything is alright
A cruel chill comes across you
Thank God for top soil….whew
From the street and morgue to the
ground
How they all depart with a devilish
frown
Cold, stiff, pale and unstuffed
When your soul leaves your body
doesn't get up
Hard, lonely and looking sick
Difficult to say goodbye to and
missed
Your flesh is so tensed and
complicated to kiss
Life, love and longevity
Filled with embalming fluid makes
you heavy

Kissed By Words:The Prelude

Flowers tombstones and much
sorrow
Got to find some black to shortly
borrow
A long cloudy drear some day
Dismal, wintry, and gloomy, God
don't take me away
Death is so atramentous so
nigrescent
Black roses are a dead man's present
When that casket drops it is evident
You are no longer here you're
irrelevant
The extinct, the rested in lovely peace
Sad singing and flower bringing for
the deceased
May god bless our souls all these long
nights
May god rest their souls who reside
at all the
Many "Grave Sights!"

"I'm Like"

I'm like a fly caught in a web
I'm like a teacher that can't spell
I'm like a fire with no heat
I'm like a shepherd with lost sheep
I'm like day-time without a noon
I'm like a night sky without a moon
I'm like a cry without tears
I'm like a car without gears
I'm like a fallen tree no one can hear
I'm like the dock at the pier and
everyone is walking on me
I'm like a seeing-eye dog that can't
see
Bare with me
I'm like an army, fighting with all its
might....
Hold on...
I'm not done telling you what "I'm
Like"

I'm like a builder who doesn't build
I'm like a schizophrenic without pills

Kissed By Words:The Prelude

I'm like Jack fallen down that hill
I'm like a pianist who don't play
I'm like night with no day
I'm like a pit bull without teeth
I'm like a beat with no beat
I'm like a hiker who doesn't hike
The world is like a sinner without
salvation
And that's not what "I'm Like"

Invisible Mailman

Something peculiar happened today
A whisper of thrill came by my way
I saw something that wasn't there
Invisible mail is really quite rare
The scent was sweet as I can recall
So sweet I smelled nothin at all
The penmanship was neat and clean
So neat that it couldn't even be seen
I'm writing you back with much love
you can bet
To thank you for the kite I didn't get
Don't worry I am not near mad
Things aren't as bad
No hard feelings aren't you glad
If I was overseas would it be better
Then maybe I could expect your
letter
Not enough hours in a day I
understand
Now I can wait patiently for the
"Invisible Mailman"

Kissed By Words:The Prelude

Jesus is Real

He is very real to me
I can feel Him in my hands
I can feel Him in my feet
I can even feel Him when I'm walking
these streets
I have come to know He is real
Because He has revealed life's truths
to me
He has given me peace at night
He has give me eternal life
I'm never alone in the devils lair
You know why (Jehovah Shammah)
the Lord is there
My Redeemer has the power to heal
And that's not all the reason Jesus is
Real

He is there to catch that fallen tear
My Comforter and that voice I hear
My soul-seeker unmistakably speaks
loud and clear

Kissed By Words:The Prelude

These of which I have boldly
mentioned
Are what makes me stand justly at
attention
When all else has seemed to have
failed
When something inside of me feels
like the depths of Hell
He lets me know I will undeniably
prevail
He has forewarned me of what the
adversary will try to steal
And that is one among many reasons
why Jesus is Real

Meditation

In a deep comatose-like state
Will my thoughts ever migrate?
They stay the same day in and day
out
I wonder what's wrong what is this all
about
Thinking hard on one thing and one
thing only
How I feel nothing but pain and I am
lonely

Can this aggression come from the
matter at hand?
When will my mind gather enough
evidence to understand?
Is my brain able to choose and obtain
an instrumentality?
Or is it possible the things I think of
will cause a fatality
My feelings and my emotions are
constantly intransigent

Kissed By Words:The Prelude

Sometimes I say things but they
aren't what I meant
The senses I have always intervene
and interpose
With not only my heart and brain but
it's cool I suppose
Because when my conscience kicks in
so does my memory
It's unbelievable the way my life has
its own true story
But for some reason I am not able o
tell it too well

First my heart tells my thoughts they
inform my mind
Then my brain starts to working and
captures them like a jail
By then I have reached and I noticed
that I am out of time

Now sit back muse and recollect is
what I tell myself
That way I will have a lot more room
for something else

Kissed By Words:The Prelude

I guess to finalize everything I'll have
to use arbitration
So sooner or later I will be able to
have complete "Meditation"

MISSANDAHOOD

The poverty, fights, hunger, and
crime rate
Sickness, basketball tournaments, but
the murders I hate
When inside our world you get a
sense of belonging
All the morning cries as well as the
midnight moaning
We all like the blues, booze and
especially the barbecue
Those things I have mentioned helps
us pull through
I seen all the buildings all closed in
lock up tight
But hey I'm living; I am free so i guess
it's alright
The block and house parties jumping
filled with glee
I just wish everyone could go there
and see what I see

Kissed By Words:The Prelude

It is not all violence sometimes we
can live peacefully
In the hot days the fire hydrants are
turned on

The only problem we have is the
outside won't leave us alone
Walking in places where there are
not any sidewalks
Abandoned houses where we watch
things like night hawks
Good Baptist churches where we get
along and have talks
We played hopscotch and played
some rough basketball
Can't forget about the penny candy
that I miss most of all
From the courts, to the fields to
shooting dice in the hall

I tried to leave but like a house pet I
found my way back
I returned because society said us
hoodlums don't know how to act

Kissed By Words:The Prelude

Any and everywhere I go I am
misunderstood
That's why I'll always be "MISSING
THE HOOD"

Questions

Did we exist before our own birth?
Why are we here on this reputable
earth?
What makes me be me?
What is really reality?
What makes you be you?
Which way do we chose
Who are we to judge?
Do I really need a hug?
What are our transgressions?
Can you give me all the answers to
these questions?
Could we give a little more?
When will opportunity knock at the
door?
What does it mean to be loved?
What if the shoe fits like a glove?
How does the time fly by?
Why do we even bother to lie?
Why do we obsess over worldly
possessions?

Can you comprehend my worded
expressions?
Why is it that we yearn for one's
affection?
Will we go into another recession?
Are these rhetorical "Questions"

Skirts

We can be taken before we get
To the place everybody calls birth
At anytime we can be taken
Away from this place that we call
earth
They make us run, chase, search and
search
So beware of that enemy we call
"Skirts"

Why do they give and take at the
same time
The way they break hearts should be
a crime
When they've wronged they act like a
mime
They bear children to hold them
against you
We can't take them through half the
things they take us through
How they do the voodoo they do

We must have them like a foot and
shoe
I guess that's what we get for being a
flirt
But still be cautious of them beings
we call "Skirts"

Pimpin

That way of living poured me a little
ambition
Living a hard knock life is a
complicated mission
A wart on the nose of humanity
This path is followed universally
At first it was like eating barbecue
Now it seems as if I was eating
mildew
This type of life lessens one's
standard
Standing on corners naked while men
gander
I never thought I would become a
pander
Soliciting is like a rocking chair
Something to do but it gets you
nowhere
Mind manipulation was the key in the
ignition

It was considered to be an outlet for
aggression
Selling those women was
dehumanization
They didn't' know it but it was
degeneration
Even though it wasn't I thought it was
Without a doubt an honest way of
livin'
Women I'm sorry for that thing we
call "Pimpin"

About The Author

I am a 32 yr old God-fearing, divorced Father of 4. A Welder/Author originally from Chicago I'll., who's had the pleasure of growing up in a small town called Cairo Ill. as well...I enjoy the simple things in life as so should you!

Greetings, family, friends, and readers! I have selected a few works from my book of Poetry to give you a glimpse of what is yet to come...Some of my writings are against the grain of American Life and some we all can relate to...I have published these works in hopes that some may gain a sense of relief knowing we all are the same situation in certain aspects, through my sorrow as well as my glee...With that said Enjoy and share with family, friends, and coworkers...Much Obliged!

Kissed By Words:The Prelude

.

www.ingramcontent.com/pod-product-compliance
Lightning Source LLC
Chambersburg PA
CBHW071850020426
42331CB00007B/1946